# ON THE BOAT
## ON THE ROAD
### and at home

## HEALTHY • EASY • DELICIOUS

#### RECIPES WITH SIMPLE INGREDIENTS

PLANT-BASED FOOD FROM THE GALLEY

# STORY
## OF THE
# BOOK

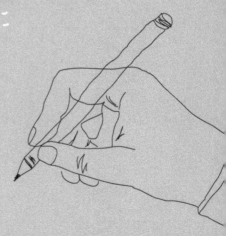

This book is dedicated to you! We are committed to showing you how easy it can be to live a better, healthier and more sustainable life. *It won't be long until you feel a difference*. Your energy will increase, your body will be in better shape, your libido will go up and your brain will be more alert.

When Judith and Wes met, he was motivated to change his lifestyle and nutrition but he didn't know where to start. He was always tired - largely because he was addicted to sugar, as many people are. Judith had been studying nutrition and sustainability for years, and was working towards her Health Coach certification; she was thrilled to share her knowledge with Wes.

With Judith's support, he changed his eating habits and after two months his sugar cravings decreased. His energy went up and he lost more than 30 lbs over four months, simply by converting to a more nutritious diet.

Judith developed recipes that are easy to prepare and easy to follow, that contain ingredients that are not too exotic and also include ideas for substitutions and options.

This was when the idea was born to write a book to help other "challenged cooks" to change their food choices from processed, low nutrient food to more sustainable, high nutrient food that is the foundation of healthy living.

After the recipe section, you will find useful tips including a mini-guide for leading a healthier lifestyle.

## Let's begin!

# CONTENTS

# How to use this book

To make it as **easy** as possible, we tried not to use exotic ingredients that may not be readily available. Often we suggest options in the recipe and also we suggest substitute ingredients in case the original is not on hand or you don't find it appealing.

The ingredients are blended into the text in a step by step fashion, so you do not have to go back and forth between ingredients and how to prepare it.

Ingredients and their quantities are in bold font. Be sure to read through the entire recipe before preparing your meal, and gather all ingredients listed.

## PANTRY STAPLES

Here is a list of **delicious ingredients** that may be **new to you** but should be in your pantry as a basic staple:

- **COCONUT MILK/CREAM IN A CAN** (NOT THE BEVERAGE IN THE TETRA PACK)
- **NUTRITIONAL YEAST**
- **CUMIN POWDER**
- **TURMERIC POWDER**
- **HIMALAYAN SALT**
- **SAGE POWDER**
- **TEMPEH** (FERMENTED SOY), PLEASE CHOOSE ORGANIC
- **COCONUT OIL** (IT'S NOT LIQUID)
- **RED LENTILS**

On page 97 you will find a list of foods we use with their nutritional benefits!

It takes about 6 to 8 weeks to change your taste preferences. After that, your **taste buds** will begin to enjoy the change. You will experience a literal **change of taste**!

## YOUR PERSONAL ANSWER

You will find that the more you choose healthy foods, the more you will like it! And the good feeling that comes with it, is actually the most important and noticeable benefit.

If you crave unhealthy food ask yourself; "WHY would I take a step back?" Or "WHY do I make healthy choices over donuts and processed meat?" Maybe you want to feel better in general; or you want to have more energy because your goal is to run a marathon; or maybe you want to live a long, joyful life with lots of adventures; maybe your goal is to get healthy to attend your grandchildren's wedding. Whatever it is, ask yourself WHY and find your **personal answer**. This is your positive anchor to help you stay committed to your goal. When you feel challenged, remind yourself of your personal answer, the why behind healthy, nutrient rich food.

## A NOTE ABOUT ORGANIC

**To eat clean without pesticides** is part of the healthy nutrition ethos. Some foods are sprayed more than others and we added "organic" to those ingredients that we highly recommend you eat organic. More about organic versus non-organic on page 103.

## GARLIC, AMAZING GARLIC

**Garlic** is one of the most beneficial plants for your health and we hope you love it as much as we do. The amount of garlic you use is entirely up to you. If you are not used to garlic, start with less than suggested. If you love garlic, double the amount if you like. If you choose to use more garlic you may reduce the amount of salt.

## GET IN TOUCH

If you get confused please feel free to email us at **info@svhakluyt.com** and we will do our best to help! If the answer takes a bit longer we might be on an ocean crossing or at a place with no service but we will try to answer as soon as we can.

## TRANSLATION COMING SOON

Although we are planning to translate this book into **German,** we added a **list of conversions** from imperial to metric for our European friends on page 96.

# soups

13

# Captain's Favourite Tomato Soup

15

# Mushroom Cream Soup

17

# Remedy Soup
### (onion/garlic/herbs)

# Captain's Favourite Tomato Soup

4 SERVINGS

8-10  FRESH (ORGANIC) TOMATOES
OR 1 LARGE CAN OF (ORGANIC) TOMATOES (800 ML)

1 CAN (2 CUPS)  COCONUT MILK

1 CAN  (ORGANIC) TOMATO PASTE (155 ML)

6-8  FRESH BASIL LEAVES (OR 1 TBSP DRIED BASIL)

1 TSP  HIMALAYAN SALT

1 TSP  OREGANO

1 TSP  PEPPER

› put everything in a blender and blend until smooth

› heat up over medium heat, stirring frequently (takes 5 - 10 minutes)

› *note: it doesn't taste great **before** it is heated!*

SUBSTITUTES

› thyme for oregano

# Mushroom Cream Soup

4 SERVINGS

10-14 LARGE MUSHROOMS (WHITE BUTTON OR CREMINI)

1 CAN COCONUT MILK

1 1/2 CUPS VEGETABLE BROTH (ORGANIC)

1/2 ONION

5-8 CLOVES OF GARLIC

1 TSP HIMALAYAN SALT

1 TSP PEPPER

1/2 TSP NUTMEG

› put all ingredients in a blender and blend until smooth

› simmer the soup in a pot on medium heat for 20 minutes, stirring frequently

SUBSTITUTES

› omit the onions

# Remedy Soup
## (onion/garlic/herb)

**4 SERVINGS**

This is the perfect soup to recover from a cold or any other sickness, especially if you have taken antibiotics. It will feed the good bacteria in your gut to heal your microbiome.

| | |
|---|---|
| 4 ONIONS | 1/2 TSP GINGER |
| 2 BULBS GARLIC | 1 TSP HIMALAYAN SALT |
| 3 STALKS CELERY | 1/2 TSP PEPPER |
| 3 CUPS WATER | 1/2 TSP CUMIN |
| 1/2 CUP FRESH HERB LIKE BASIL OR THYME | 1/2 TSP SAGE POWDER |

› put all ingredients in a pot and simmer at medium heat for 20 minutes, stirring frequently

› blend in a glass blender or with a hand blender

SUBSTITUTES

› 2 more onions for garlic

› oregano for sage powder

# ONE
## MEAL
## ONE
## PAN

### THE EASIEST MEALS
### FOR REALLY BAD COOKS

# Mushroom Dahlsotto

4 SERVINGS

1 CAN  COCONUT MILK

4-5 CUPS  WATER

2 CUPS  RED LENTILS (UNCOOKED)

6-10  CLOVES GARLIC, MINCED

1 ONION, CHOPPED

1 TBSP  APPLE CIDER VINEGAR

1 1/2 CUPS  MUSHROOMS, SLICED
(ANY MUSHROOM WORKS)

1 TSP  TURMERIC

1 TSP  CUMIN

2 TSP  HIMALAYAN SALT

1/2 TSP  GINGER

1/2 TSP  PEPPER

CHILI OR CAYENNE PEPPER
TO TASTE

› put everything in a pot and simmer for 30 minutes on medium heat
  or until lentils are soft, almost mashy

› add water if needed and stir frequently

SUBSTITUTES

› brown or green lentils for red lentils (need to boil longer)

› curry for turmeric

› omit mushrooms and have just a dahl

# Tomato Sauce with Pasta

**4 SERVINGS**

*This recipe is perfect for camping when you only have one burner available.*
*Use half of each ingredient for a small camping cooker.*

**1 LARGE CAN TOMATOES (ORGANIC) 800ML**

**4 CUPS WATER**

**1 CUP RED LENTILS**

**1 ONION, CHOPPED**

**2 CUPS RICE PASTA, LENTIL PASTA OR CHICKPEA PASTA**

**2 TSP HIMALAYAN SALT**

**1 TSP PEPPER**

**2 TSP OREGANO**

**5-8 CLOVES OF GARLIC, CHOPPED**

› put in a pot and boil on medium heat for 30 minutes or until pasta is soft, stir frequently

› add:

   **4 TBSP NUTRITIONAL YEAST**

   **HOT CHILLI OR CAYENNE PEPPER TO TASTE**

› enjoy with your favourite salad at your favourite campsite!

SUBSTITUTES

› thyme or basil for oregano

# Veggie Casserole

**4 SERVINGS**

› preheat the oven to 400° F

› fill your (medium size) casserole with your favourite veggies such as:
 **BROCCOLI, CAULIFLOWER, SPINACH (ORGANIC), ZUCCHINI, CARROTS, SWEET POTATOES, GREEN BEANS, ANY ROOT VEGETABLE, KALE (ORGANIC), CHARD (ORGANIC), BRUSSEL SPROUTS, MUSHROOMS, GARLIC, ONIONS OR LEEK**

› if you would like to add **POTATOES (ORGANIC)** you have to pre-boil them for 15 minutes

› make the sauce:
 **1 CAN COCONUT MILK**   **2 TSP HIMALAYAN SALT**
 **1 TSP PEPPER**   **1 TSP NUTMEG**
 **4 TBSP NUTRITIONAL YEAST**

› whisk in a bowl and pour over the veggies

› bake in the oven for 40 minutes or until veggies are tender

› serve with rice or quinoa

**SUBSTITUTES**

› cumin for nutmeg

# Galley Lentils

4 SERVINGS

1 ONION, CHOPPED

1 SMALL LEEK, CHOPPED

5-8 CLOVES OF GARLIC, MINCED

1 1/2 CUPS UNCOOKED RED LENTILS

1 CAN (2 CUPS) COCONUT MILK

1 CAN TOMATO PASTE (155 ML)

4 CUPS WATER

1 TBSP APPLE CIDER VINEGAR

2 TSP HIMALAYAN SALT

1 1/2 TSP SAGE POWDER

1 1/2 TSP TURMERIC

1/2 TSP BLACK PEPPER

1 TSP CUMIN

HOT CHILLI POWDER TO TASTE

› put everything in a pot and bring to a boil

› turn heat to low and simmer for 20 minutes or until lentils are soft and creamy

› stir frequently and add water if needed

SUBSTITUTES

› more leek for celery

› more onion for leek

› more leek for onion

› thyme or basil for sage

# Baked Potatoes

**2 SERVINGS**

› preheat the oven to 400° F

› wash, cut in wedges and put in a bowl:

   **4  MEDIUM SIZE POTATOES (ORGANIC)**

› then add:

   **4 TBSP  AVOCADO OIL OR GRAPE SEED OIL**

   **1 TSP  HIMALAYAN SALT**

   **1/2 TSP  PEPPER**

› stir the ingredients together and spread them on a baking sheet

› bake for 40 - 45 minutes

› serve with **PESTO** (page 69) or **MAYO** (page 71)

› serve with a **SALAD** to add more vitamins and minerals!

SUBSTITUTES

› sweet potatoes or any other veggie for potatoes

# SALADS

AND

## DRESSINGS

# How to create the salad you love

There are so many vegetables, seeds, nuts and much more you can create a salad with! We will leave it up to you to put the salad together. It is simple ... it's like ordering a pizza with the toppings you like!

Choose from the following ingredients
and add your favourite dressing (pages 39 to 47):

- **LEAVES (ALL SHOULD BE ORGANIC)**

  kale, iceberg, romaine, chard, spinach, arugula, dandelion

- **VEGGIES**

  carrots, peppers (organic), avocado, cucumber, tomatoes (organic), cabbage, onions, sweet potatoes and other roots vegetables

- **FRUITS**

  apples (organic), mangos, berries (organic), pineapple

- **RAW OR COOKED**

  broccoli, brussel sprouts, green beans, sweet potatoes, cauliflower

- **FRESH HERBS**

  cilantro, parsley, basil (all organic)

- **SPROUTS**

  sprouts or micro-greens are one of the healthiest foods in the world.

- **LEGUMES (COOKED)**

  chickpeas, black beans, lentils, kidney beans, faba beans

- **NUTS AND SEEDS**

  pumpkin seeds, hemp seeds, walnuts, almonds, sesame seeds, sunflower seeds

- **ADD ONE OR MORE OF THESE TO MAKE A BIG MEAL OUT OF YOUR SALAD:**

  cooked quinoa, boiled or baked potato (organic), fried/boiled mushrooms and/or tempeh (this is our favourite – see recipe on page 37).

green beans, leafy greens, peppers, **broccoli sprouts,** avocado, pumpkin seeds, cabbage

**Leafy greens, carrots, blueberries, onions, mixed sprouts, pumpkin seeds, cabbage**

**Leafy greens, broccoli, oranges, pumpkin seeds**

# Fried-Boiled Mushrooms and Tempeh

Here is an idea on how to fry-boil:

› cut **MUSHROOMS** and **TEMPEH (ORGANIC)** in small pieces

› put **2-3 TBSP  COCONUT OIL** and **1/4 CUP  OF WATER** in a pot,
   add a dash of **HIMALAYAN SALT,  MUSHROOMS** and **TEMPEH**
   and cook the mix for 10 minutes and top your salad with it

# Yellow Submarine
## (turmeric dressing)

4 SERVINGS

4-5 CLOVES GARLIC, MINCED

1/4 CUP OLIVE OIL*

1/4 CUP AVOCADO OIL OR COLD
PRESSED GRAPE SEED OIL*

1/4 CUP WATER

1 TSP HIMALAYAN SALT

1 TSP TURMERIC

1/2 TSP PEPPER

HOT CHILLI POWDER TO TASTE

1 1/2 TBSP APPLE CIDER VINEGAR

1/2 SMALL CARROT, CUT IN PIECES

1/2 CUP SOY MILK (ORGANIC)

› put all ingredients in a blender and blend until smooth

* replace one of the oils with flax seed oil or hempseed oil. Both are very rich in alpha-linolenic acid (omega-3 essential fatty acid). Omega-3 is essential for brain health and it increases the level of leptin, the hormone that tells you that you are full (great for weight loss!)

SUBSTITUTES

› water for soy milk

› omit carrot

› any vinegar for apple cider vinegar

# Hakluyt's Garlic Buzz

**4 SERVINGS**

8-12  CLOVES GARLIC, PRESSED

1/4 CUP  OLIVE OIL*

1/4 CUP  AVOCADO OIL*

1/4 CUP  WATER

1 TBSP  APPLE CIDER VINEGAR

1/2 TSP  HIMALAYAN SALT

1/2 TSP  PEPPER

2 TBSP  NUTRITIONAL YEAST

OPTIONAL: 1 TBSP  FRESH HERBS LIKE BASIL, THYME OR OREGANO

› press the garlic into a small bowl

› add all other ingredients and whisk for 10 seconds

*replace one of the oils with flaxseed oil or hemp seed oil. Both are very rich in alpha-linolenic acid (omega-3 essential fatty acid). Omega 3 is essential for brain health and it increases the level of leptin, the hormone that tells you that you are full (great for weight loss).*

SUBSTITUTES

› omit nutritional yeast and call it only "garlic buzz"

# Red Island
## (apple ginger dressing)

4 SERVINGS

| | |
|---|---|
| 1/2 SMALL APPLE | 1 TSP PEPPER |
| 1 SMALL CARROT | 5-6 CLOVES GARLIC |
| 2 TBSP AVOCADO OIL* | 1 1/2 TSP GINGER |
| 2 TBSP OLIVE OIL* | 1 TSP TURMERIC |
| 1/3 CUP WATER | 2 TSP APPLE CIDER VINEGAR |
| 1 TSP HIMALAYAN SALT | 3 TBSP NUTRITIONAL YEAST |

› put in a blender and blend until smooth

› add water if too thick

*replace one of the oils with flaxseed oil or hemp seed oil. Both are very rich in alpha-linolenic acid (omega-3 essential fatty acid). Omega 3 is essential for brain health and it increases the level of leptin, the hormone that tells you that you are full (great for weight loss).*

SUBSTITUTES

› mango for apple

# Green Ocean
## (avocado dressing)

4 SERVINGS

1/2 AVOCADO

4 CLOVES GARLIC

3 TBSP AVOCADO OIL*

2 TBSP OLIVE OIL*

1 TSP APPLE CIDER VINEGAR

1/2 CUP WATER

1 TBSP DRIED OR FRESH CILANTRO (ORGANIC)

1/2 TSP HIMALAYAN SALT

1/2 TSP PEPPER

1/2 TSP CRUSHED PEPPER (OPTIONAL)

› put all ingredients in a blender and blend until smooth

*replace one of the oils with flaxseed oil or hemp seed oil. Both are very rich in alpha-linolenic acid (omega-3 essential fatty acid). Omega 3 is essential for brain health and it increases the level of leptin, the hormone that tells you that you are full (great for weight loss).*

SUBSTITUTES

› any vinegar for apple cider vinegar

› basil for cilantro

# We call it "Honey"
## (date mustard dressing)

4 SERVINGS

3 DATES
*soak in 1/3 cup water for 3 hours or overnight*

3 CLOVES GARLIC

1/4 CUP  AVOCADO OIL*

1/4 CUP  OLIVE OIL*

2 TBSP  MUSTARD

2 TSP  VINEGAR

1 TSP  HIMALAYAN SALT

1/2 TSP  PEPPER

1/2 TSP  CRUSHED PEPPER

DASH OF TURMERIC FOR THE COLOUR (OPTIONAL)

› put all ingredients in a blender (including the date water) and blend until smooth

*\* replace one of the oils with flaxseed oil or hemp seed oil. Both are very rich in alpha-linolenic acid (omega-3 essential fatty acid). Omega 3 is essential for brain health and it increases the level of leptin, the hormone that tells you that you are full (great for weight loss).*

SUBSTITUTES

› 2 tbsp maple syrup or coconut sugar for dates

# MAIN

# COURSES

51

# Pizza Pie

55

# "Sneat"
## Stuffed Mushrooms/Peppers

59

# Dutch Shepherd's Pie

61

# Mushroom-Tempeh Gravy
## (with rice or quinoa)

63

# Mom's German
# Potato Salad

# Pizza Pie

MAKES ONE PIZZA

› preheat oven to 420° F

› (CRUST)

1 CAN OF CHICKPEAS (400 ML)
(OR 2 CUPS BOILED CHICKPEAS)

1/2 CUP SPELT FLOUR
(OR BUCKWHEAT FLOUR FOR THE
GLUTEN FREE VERSION OF THE
PIZZA PIE)

1 TSP OREGANO

1 TSP HIMALAYAN SALT

1/4 CUP AVOCADO
OR GRAPE SEED OIL

1/2 CUP WATER

› put in a blender and mix until it's a very thick batter

› add water if needed

› spread it on a small baking sheet with parchment paper, a round pizza pan
or a pizza stone (that's what we use)

› bake for 15 minutes at 420° F before adding toppings

*note: spelt flour holds the crust together much better than buckwheat flour
but buckwheat flour makes this dish gluten free!*

# Pizza Pie

› meanwhile make the **TOMATO SAUCE:**

**1 SMALL CAN OF DICED TOMATOES (ORGANIC)**

**2 TBSP TOMATO PASTE (ORGANIC)**

**1/2 TSP HIMALAYAN SALT**

**1/2 TSP PEPPER**

**1 TSP THYME OR OREGANO**

› put in a blender and blend until smooth

› spread tomato sauce on the pre-baked crust, don't overfill the crust, you may have leftovers

› add your **FAVOURITE TOPPINGS** like:

**ONIONS, PINEAPPLE, MUSHROOMS, TOMATOES, PEPPERS (ORGANIC), HOT PEPPERS, OLIVES, SNEAT (PLANT-BASED MEAT, PAGE 55)**

› put it back in the oven and bake for 15 minutes

› then add **SPINACH OR KALE (IF DESIRED)** and **PLANT-BASED CHEESE (PAGE 73)** and bake for another 5 - 8 minutes

› serve with a salad

# "Sneat"

4 SERVINGS

## 's not meat but tastes much better – stuffed mushrooms and peppers or sneat balls*

› preheat oven to 400° F, cover a baking tray with parchment paper

› boil for about 30 minutes or until lentils are soft:

1 CUP  BROWN OR GREEN LENTILS with

2 1/2 CUPS  WATER

2 BAY  LEAVES

› cool, take the bay leaves out and put lentils in a blender and blend for 1 - 2 seconds or use the fork to mash them, then put them in a bowl

› then add:

1 1/2 CUPS  WALNUTS, ROUGHLY GROUND

1 TBSP  AVOCADO OR GRAPE SEED OIL

1 TSP  CUMIN

1 TSP  SAGE POWDER

1 TSP  HIMALAYAN SALT

6  CLOVES GARLIC (PRESSED)

A DASH  HOT CHILI OR CAYENNE PEPPER (TO TASTE)

1 CUP  SHREDDED MUSHROOM (OPTIONAL)

1 CUP  SHREDDED ONIONS (OPTIONAL)

› add to the bowl and mix with a fork

› **10 BIG WHITE BUTTON MUSHROOMS OR 4 PORTOBELLO**

› take stems out and hollow out

› and cut:
  **3 BELL PEPPERS (ANY COLOUR) (ORGANIC)**

› in half and take the seeds out

› stuff the mushrooms and/or peppers with sneat

› then add a layer of:
  **VEGAN CHEESE (PAGE 73)**

› place on baking sheet

› bake in the oven for 30 - 35 minutes at 400° F

*instead of stuffing veggies with sneat, you can roll them and serve as sneat balls!
Roll little balls in your palms and place on parchment covered sheet.
Bake for 30 - 35 minutes. Can be added to a salad, or enjoyed with Mushroom-Tempeh
Gravy (page 61).*

SUBSTITUTES

› pecan nuts for walnuts

› red lentils for brown/green lentils

› basil for thyme

› hollowed zucchini for mushroom and pepper

› more mushrooms for peppers

› more peppers for mushrooms

› omit the bay leaves

# Dutch Shepherd's Pie

4 SERVINGS

› preheat oven to 400° F, cover a baking tray with parchment paper

› **5-6 LARGE POTATOES (ORGANIC)**

› peel, cut in quarters and boil them until tender

› then drain most of the water, leave around 1 cup water in the pot and add
  **3 TBSP  COCONUT OIL**
  **1 CUP  SOY, OAT OR NUT MILK**
  **1 TSP  HIMALAYAN SALT**
  **1/2 TSP  NUTMEG**

› mash and set aside

| | |
|---|---|
| 1 CUP RED LENTILS | 4-5 LEAVES CHARD, CUT IN STRIPS |
| 2 CUPS WATER | 2 TSP HIMALAYAN SALT |
| 10-12 CHOPPED MUSHROOMS | 1 TSP PEPPER |
| 1 LARGE ONION, DICED | 2 TSP SAGE POWDER |
| 1 ZUCCHINI, DICED | OR 1/2 CUP FRESH SAGE LEAVES |
| 1 CAN COCONUT MILK | 1 TSP CUMIN |
| 8 CLOVES GARLIC, MINCED | 1 TSP TURMERIC |

› put in a pot and boil on medium heat for 30 minutes

› place the stew in a casserole dish and carefully spread the mashed potatoes on top

› put in the oven and bake at 400° F for 30 - 40 minutes
  (or until potatoes are very slightly browning)


SUBSTITUTES:

› thyme for sage

› kale or spinach for chard

# Mushroom - Tempeh Gravy
## (served with rice pasta, potatoes or quinoa)

4 SERVINGS

1 CAN  COCONUT MILK

3 CUPS  SLICED SHIITAKE, CREMINI
OR WHITE BUTTON MUSHROOMS

1/2  RED OR WHITE ONION, CHOPPED

1 PACKAGE TEMPEH (ORGANIC),
CUT IN SMALL PIECES

1/2 TSP  HIMALAYAN SALT

1/4 TSP  PEPPER

1/4 TSP  NUTMEG

› put everything in a pot and simmer for 25 minutes

› serve with mashed potatoes, rice, quinoa or pasta

SUBSTITUTES:

› more onions for mushrooms

› tofu for tempeh

# Mom's German potato salad

3-4 SERVINGS

› **4-5  LARGE POTATOES (ORGANIC)**

› cover with water

› boil for 30 minutes or until tender and let them sit for a few hours to cool

› peel the skin off and slice potatoes very thinly and put into a bowl and add

| | |
|---|---|
| **1/2 CUP  MAYO (PAGE 71)** | **1 TSP  VINEGAR** |
| **1 TSP  HIMALAYAN SALT** | **1 TBSP  OLIVE OIL** |
| **1/2 TSP  PEPPER** | **1/2  SWEET ONION, CHOPPED (OPTIONAL)** |
| **2 TSP  PAPRIKA** | |

› and carefully mix in with the potatoes

› decorate with herbs and/or cucumbers or tomatoes (organic)

› *best served when left in the fridge overnight!!!*

SUBSTITUTES:

› sorry no substitutes here

# DIPS,
# SAUCES
# AND
# CHEESE

# Judith's Addictive Hummus

MAKES ~7 CUPS

2 CANS  (400 ML PER CAN) CHICKPEAS
(GARBANZO BEANS)
OR 4 CUPS  BOILED CHICKPEAS

1/4 CUP  AVOCADO OIL

1/4 CUP  OLIVE OIL OR HEMP SEED OIL

1 CUP  WATER

2 TSP  FRESH LEMON JUICE

2 TBSP  ALMOND BUTTER

10-15  CLOVES GARLIC
(REAL PIRATES USE 20)

1 1/2 TSP  HIMALAYAN SALT

1 TSP  PEPPER

2 TSP  TURMERIC

CAYENNE PEPPER TO TASTE

› put all ingredients in a blender and blend until smooth

› decorate with some red crushed pepper flakes or herbs

SUBSTITUTES

› peanut butter or tahini for almond butter

› apple cider vinegar for lemon juice

# Crew's Favourite Pesto

MAKES 3 1/2 CUPS

› **3/4 CUP CASHEW NUTS**

› soak for 30 minutes or more

› put in a blender and add:

**10 CLOVES GARLIC**

**1 CUP AVOCADO OIL**

**1/2 CUP OLIVE OIL**

**1 CUP FRESH BASIL LEAVES**

**1 TBSP FRESH LEMON JUICE**

**1/2 TSP HIMALAYAN SALT**

**1/2 TSP BLACK PEPPER**

**3-4 TBSP NUTRITIONAL YEAST**

› blend for 2 - 3 minutes

SUBSTITUTES

› apple cider vinegar for lemon juice

› cilantro for basil

# First Mate's Favourite Mayo

MAKES 3 CUPS

1 CUP  SOY MILK (ORGANIC)

2 CUPS  GRAPE SEED OIL

1 TSP  HIMALAYAN SALT

DASH BLACK PEPPER

1 TSP  FRESH LEMON JUICE

› put in a blender and blend for a few seconds until thick

› **optional:** add a few cloves of garlic to make it a garlic mayo

SUBSTITUTES

› apple cider vinegar for lemon juice

› avocado oil for grape seed oil

› DO NOT replace the soy milk with nut milk, it simply doesn't work

# Plant-based cheese

MAKES 3 CUPS

1 CUP  CASHEW NUTS

6 TBSP  WATER

› soak for 30 minutes

› then put in a blender and add:

3/4 CUP  AVOCADO OIL OR
GRAPE SEED OIL

1 TSP  HIMALAYAN SALT

3 TSP  FRESH LEMON JUICE

4 TBSP  NUTRITIONAL YEAST

PEPPER TO TASTE

DASH OF TURMERIC FOR
THE COLOUR (OPTIONAL)

› add more water and a dash of salt if you want it more liquid
and less water to make it more firm

SUBSTITUTES

› apple cider vinegar for lemon juice

› pumpkin seeds for cashews, soak them overnight

# Captain's Guacamole

MAKES 3 CUPS

› 3 AVOCADOS

› mash with a fork

› add:

    1/2 RED ONION, DICED

    1/2 TSP HIMALAYAN SALT

    1/2 TSP PEPPER

    9-10 CLOVES GARLIC, MINCED

    4 STICKS GREEN ONIONS, CHOPPED

    3/4 CUP FRESH CILANTRO

    1/2 TSP CUMIN

    1/2 FRESH DICED TOMATO (ORGANIC)

    1 TBSP LIME JUICE

SUBSTITUTES

› lemon juice or apple cider vinegar for lime juice and call it "weird guacamole"

# SWEETS & CAKES

# Chocolate Walnut Cake
## with health benefits

6-8 SERVINGS

> ( CRUST )

   **16 DATES (AMOUNT FOR THE ENTIRE CAKE)**

   **1 1/2 CUPS CASHEW NUTS**

› soak both separately for 1 - 2 hours

› **1 CUP OF THE SOAKED CASHEW NUTS**

   **6 OF THE SOAKED DATES**

› put both in a blender with some of the date water to get a nice paste
   and put in a bowl

› add:

   **1 CUP SHREDDED WALNUTS**

   **1/2 TSP CINNAMON**

   **2 TBSP MELTED COCONUT OIL**

› mix in with a fork

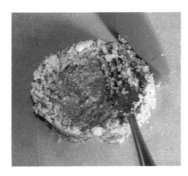

› form 6 - 8 little crusts (see image) or one large crust

› put in the freezer until cream is ready

## NOW PREPARE THE CREAM:

Note: not all coconut milk will work for this. You need one where the milk and fat are separated, to use the solidified part (the fat) only. A brand that works well is Native Forest.

› 1/2 CAN COCONUT MILK (ONLY THE SOLID PART!)

1 AVOCADO

6 OF THE SOAKED DATES

3 TBSP RAW CACAO

3 TBSP MELTED COCONUT OIL

› in a blender with some of the dates water and blend until smooth

› add the cream to the crusts and put back in the freezer

### › ICING:

1/2 CUP OF THE SOAKED CASHEWS

3 TBSP MELTED COCONUT OIL

4 OF THE SOAKED DATES (INCLUDING SOME OF THE DATE WATER)

1/2 TSP ALMOND EXTRACT

› put in a blender and blend until smooth

› add on top of the cream

› put back in the freezer for about 15 more minutes before you enjoy them

You may keep the little cakes in the freezer and take them out about 30 minutes before you want to eat them. Great to have as a snack or if guests unexpectedly visit.

SUBSTITUTES

› shredded coconut or pecans for walnuts in crust

# Almond Chocolate

**12 PIECES**

› cover a baking sheet with parchment paper and set aside

› **7 DATES, CHOPPED IN TINY PIECES**
  **3/4 CUP ALMONDS, CHOPPED**

› remove pits from the dates, cut in tiny pieces and put in a bowl

› stir in nuts, set aside

› **3 TBSP COCONUT OIL**

› put in a pan and melt slowly on low heat

› add:
  **3 TBSP ALMOND BUTTER**
  **2 TBSP CACAO**

› stir until smooth and creamy

› add cream to the dates and almonds

› spread about 1/2 inch thick on a baking sheet with parchment paper
  (it won't cover the entire sheet, the batter should be thick enough to not run)

› put in the freezer for a few hours

› cut or break in pieces before you enjoy


SUBSTITUTES

› omit dates and sweeten to taste with coconut sugar
› works with all kind of nuts

# Chia Banana Pudding

2 SERVINGS

› put in a blender:

  **1 CUP  SOY OR NUT MILK**

  **1  SOFT BANANA**

  **3 TBSP  CHIA SEEDS**

  **1 TBSP  COCONUT SUGAR OR MAPLE SYRUP**

  **1 TBSP  FRESHLY SQUEEZED LEMON JUICE (OPTIONAL)**

› blend for one minute

› pour into jars or bowls and put in the fridge for 1 hour

› decorate with fruit such as berries, banana, orange, apple, pineapple, mango or whatever you fancy

SUBSTITUTES

› mango for banana

# Chocolate Pudding

4 SERVINGS

› **6 DATES**

› soaked for 2 - 4 hours (depending on how soft they already are)

› put in a blender and add:

**1/2 CAN COCONUT MILK (SOLID PART ONLY \*)**

**4 TBSP CACAO**

**2 TBSP MELTED COCONUT OIL**

**1 AVOCADO**

› blend until smooth

› put in the fridge for 2 hours

› decorate with raw cacao nips

*\* note: not all coconut milk will work for this. You need one where the milk and fat are separated, to use the solidified part (the fat) only. A brand that works well is Native Forest.*

SUBSTITUTES

› omit the avocado and add another cup of coconut cream

# BREADS
------ AND ------
# BUNS

# Hakluyt's Wicked Bread

**ONE LOAF**

› DO NOT preheat the oven!

› **450 ML  LUKEWARM WATER**

› in a big bowl, then add:

   **2 TSP  INSTANT YEAST**

› whisk until it foams

› set aside

› put in a separate bowl:

   **200 G  (ORGANIC) SPELT FLOUR**

   **100 G  BUCKWHEAT FLOUR**

   **2 TSP  HIMALAYAN SALT**

› add to the yeast water:

   **2 TBSP  APPLE CIDER VINEGAR**

› add the flour mixture one spoon at a time while stirring the yeast water

› then add and work in:

**200 G (ORGANIC) OATS**

**200 G WALNUTS**

› put your dough into a 9 inch square baking pan

(you may put a layer of parchment paper in the form for easier removal)

› place in the oven

› now you can turn on the oven to 400° F and bake for 1 hour!

› let cool for at least 1 hour before removing it from the pan

### SUBSTITUTES

› spelt flour for buckwheat flour

› flax seeds or pumpkin seeds for walnuts

› Note:

For this recipe you need a scale. The exact measurement is important for a successful outcome.

This recipe is probably the most difficult in this book.

  PLEASE SEND US A NOTE AFTER CLICKING ON THE "SUBSCRIBE" BUTTON ON OUR WEBSITE (WWW.SVHAKLUYT.COM) AND WE WILL DO OUR BEST TO GET BACK TO YOU WHEN WE HAVE A GOOD INTERNET CONNECTION!

# Rosemary Buns

**6 BUNS**

› *super easy and fast!!*

› preheat oven to 400° F

› **2 CUPS  SPELT FLOUR**

  **1 CUP  WATER**

  **1 TSP  BAKING POWDER**

  **1 TSP  HIMALAYAN SALT**

  **2 TSP  ROSEMARY**

  **4 TBSP  AVOCADO OR GRAPE SEED OIL**

› put all ingredients in a bowl and mix with a fork

› with a spoon and the fork make 6 dollops on a baking sheet

› bake in the oven for 30 minutes

**SUBSTITUTES**

› cumin seeds, oregano or thyme for rosemary

# CONVERSIONS
## FOR CUPS INTO ML AND G

1 CUP LIQUID (ANYTHING) ----------------------- 327 ml

1 CUP SPELT FLOUR ------------------------------ 130 g

1 CUP WHEAT FLOUR ----------------------------- 160 g

1 CUP RED LENTILS RAW ------------------------- 175 g

1 CUP BROWN LENTILS RAW ---------------------- 185 g

1 CUP PASTA ------------------------------------- 100 g

1 CUP BROWN RICE ------------------------------ 180 g

1 CUP CASHEWS --------------------------------- 120 g

1 CUP WALNUTS --------------------------------- 120 g

1 CUP SHREDDED COCONUT ---------------------- 70 g

1 CUP COOKED LENTILS ------------------------- 250 g

1 CUP OATS ------------------------------------- 100 g

# Nutritional benefits of foods

Food is a sensory experience, we are drawn in by its' smell, visual appeal and of course the taste is full of enjoyment. Hidden behind all of that are the nutritional benefits of food, the components such as proteins, vitamins, minerals, fibre and healthy fats, that allow the body to function at its best.

Here is a quick summary of the benefits of some of our favourite ingredients listed in this book.

- **APPLE CIDER VINEGAR** helps to digest protein and prevents bloating.

- **BERRIES** are anti-angiogenic, anti-carcinogenic and antioxidant, which promotes the shrinkage of tumours. Berries are used in natural cancer treatments and cancer prevention.

- **COCONUT OIL** is rich in medium-chain triglycerides and lauric acid which is antiviral and anti-fungal, reduces the risk of heart disease, supports thyroid function, protects against alcohol damage to the liver, rejuvenates skin and prevents wrinkles.

- **CRUCIFEROUS VEGETABLES** such as broccoli, cauliflower and kale are high in isothiocynantes which help prevent cancer, promote apoptosis (cancer cell death), are anti-angiogenic, help with removal of estrogen, promote weight loss, are anti-inflammatory and antioxidant.

- **FLAX SEED OIL OR HEMPSEED OIL** are both very rich in alpha-linolenic acid (omega 3 essential fatty acid). Adding one or both of these oils makes a dressing even healthier than it already is. Omega 3 is essential for brain health and it increases the level of leptin, the hormone that tells you that you are full (great for weight loss!).

- **GARLIC AND ONIONS** are rich in organosulfur compounds which help decrease inflammation and support the immune system. They are anti-fungal, lower blood pressure, lower cholesterol and blood sugar levels to prevent or reverse diabetes and heart disease, and help healing from cancer.

- **LEGUMES** are a great source of protein, as well as resistant starch and fibre. Resistant starch and fibre feed the good bacteria in your gut to support a healthy microbiome.

- **MUSHROOMS** contain beta-glucan which is great to control blood glucose, helps with insulin resistance, and weight loss. They also contain compounds that support the growth of brain cells and protect them from damage. They help lower estrogen and are anti-angiogenic.

- **PEPPER** contains minerals including chromium, zinc and selenium.

- **HOT CHILI OR CAYENNE PEPPER** have even more of the minerals found in pepper, plus vitamin C + A.

- **TURMERIC** is anti-inflammatory and anti-carcinogenic.

# MINI GUIDE
## for a healthy lifestyle

- Eat a **diversity of fresh foods** everyday, like garlic, onions, cruciferous vegetables, leafy greens, red vegetables, root vegetables, fresh fruits and berries, tempeh and tofu, mushrooms, nuts and seeds, lentils and beans, sprouts.

- Buy organic or at least choose from the "**clean fifteen**" published by the Environmental Working Group (ewg.org).

- Sweeten with dates, coconut sugar or pure maple syrup.

- Use Himalayan salt or sea salt rather than regular table salt.

- Choose **good oils** like avocado oil, grapeseed oil and coconut oil for cooking, and olive oil, nut oils or seed oils for salads.

- Choose non-dairy products like nut or soy milk, cashew or coconut yoghurt and try our recipe for **plant-based** cheese (page 73).

- Drink water as your main beverage. Tea is great as well, especially green tea.

- Reduce your stress; consider meditation and spending time in nature.

- Exercise!!!! So important, feels so good and it's **fun** to try a new sport.

- Use **non-toxic** body care, make-up and detergents.

- Avoid sugar, wheat, refined and processed foods, and additives.

- We recommend not consuming meat or meat products but if you do, please choose organic, grass-fed and free range. Do not eat pork! Consider reducing meat - this is one of the most important decisions you can make to **benefit your health**, positively affect the planet, and improve the quality of life of animals.

- Fish from the ocean may be highly contaminated with heavy metals; the bigger the fish the more contaminated it is. Farmed fish can be full of antibiotics and may not be the healthiest choice either. Even though fish has some great **nutritional value**, the impact of over fishing and ocean pollution cannot be overstated. Not consuming fish is a big impact decision along with not eating meat.

- Don't make alcohol a daily thing, best to avoid it.

- Do not use a microwave and reduce cellphone radiation.

- **Make life fun and love unconditionally**!!!

# Does it have to be organic?

Not always... there are a few foods that are not heavily sprayed and are safe to source as non-organic. For instance: garlic, onions, avocado, mushrooms, asparagus, pineapple.

**It is important to source the following foods as organic:**

spinach, kale, tomatoes, potatoes, blueberries, strawberries, apples, peaches, nectarines, celery, lettuce, grapes, cherries, pears, bell and hot peppers and chard. These foods are heavily sprayed with pesticides, herbicides and fungicides. Most of these chemicals are detrimental to the environment in both the short and long term and many are known to cause serious health problems in humans including cancer.

For a full list of foods you can source organically and non-organically you can reference: **www.ewg.org.** Look for The Dirty Dozen and The Clean Fifteen.

Buying organic whenever possible reduces your own exposure to these chemicals and supports organic farming, which reduces the use of chemicals in agriculture in general. We hold a lot of power in what we consume - choose wisely to help make the world a healthier and happier place.

# General substitutes

Switching to a more nutrient rich diet is easier now than ever before; more plant-based milk alternatives are widely available and alternatives to non-refined sugar sweetened products.

**Here are some simple substitutions you can make:**

**CHEESE –** This can be a difficult addiction to let go of, BUT there are great alternatives out there for easy homemade plant based cheese. You can find a quick example on page 73.

**DAIRY –** There are a variety of "non-dairy" milks such as organic soy, almond, or oat milk, that make delicious dairy milk substitutes. Try canned coconut milk instead of dairy cream for your sauces, deserts, or soups.

**MEAT –** We realize this is a big one... if you want to start right now in contributing to the reduction of environmental impacts, forgoing commercial meat (and fish) products is the number one choice you can make to have a major impact. Surprisingly, plant based proteins are healthier for you than animal proteins. Plants contain all amino acids (protein building blocks), fibre, vitamins, minerals and fats your body requires. Try a mixture of beans, nuts, lentils, quinoa, chickpeas, and / or whole grains, with a diversity of vegetables and mushrooms for your complete protein source. Tofu and tempeh are both rich in protein and make excellent texture replacements. Try our recipe of homemade meat "**sneat**" (page 55).

**REFINED GRAINS** – (e.g. white flour, white bread, white rice) can be replaced with organic whole grain flours (preferably organic spelt flour). To replace store bought white bread, try "organic ancient grain, 100% whole grain bread" now commonly found in grocery stores or try our recipe of Hakluyt's wicked bread! Instead of white rice, try brown rice or quinoa, which are more flavourful and contain more fibre and protein.

**SALT** – Common household salt is not the healthiest choice. Of all the substitutes, this is by far and away the easiest! Try Himalayan or sea salt as a simple, healthy substitute.

**SUGAR and ARTIFICIAL SWEETENERS** – These are the number one cravings for most people and are found in almost every processed food product you pluck from the store shelf. But there is a multitude of healthy alternatives to "sugars / sweeteners" to give you the sweetness you crave but without all the negative effects of refined or processed sugars and artificial sweeteners (aka chemicals). Why not try coconut sugar or organic maple syrup and make this your favourite coffee sweetener? This is but one example of a "substitute". For baking cakes or making deserts try medjool dates (best soaked overnight in water to soften them up) instead of sugar.

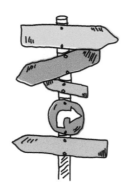

# If you have a question

on how to substitute ingredients for your favourite dish,
please send us a note after clicking on the
"subscribe" button on our website

## WWW.SVHAKLUYT.COM

and we will do our best to get back to you
when we have a good internet connection!

# Sailing Vessel Hakluyt Adventures

*Our multi-year project aims to bring awareness and education to two distinct global concerns, climate/environmental change and sustainable nutrition. To reach the mission objectives, we will utilize multiple strategies, hoping to inspire others and provide information to support positive change.*

Living a healthy lifestyle and eating clean may sound difficult to some. By starting with only a few changes and adding more nutritious foods with every recipe you try from this book, the shift to a healthier lifestyle can unfold with ease.

If we can make easy, delicious and low environmental impact meals on the boat – in remote places, for weeks and months on end – you can do this anywhere in the world. We aim to lead by example and demonstrate just how **easily** this can be done.

CHECK OUR WEBSITE
WWW.SVHAKLUYT.COM
FOR TIPS FOR A HEALTHIER LIFESTYLE
AND NEW RECIPES!

77.1932°N,
72.7182°W

77.1332°N,
72.7082°W

77.1632°N,
72.7982°W

77.1832°N,
72.7282°W

77.1332°N,
72.7082°W

# What's next?

*This book is an introduction to what will follow...*

Our next book is already planned and will not only include new, awesome and surprisingly easy-to-cook meals, but also international recipes; recipes for children; how to sprout and make yoghurt; how to make healthy homemade chips, crackers, cookies, smoothies and juices. The book will also go deeper into the **science of nutrition** to help you understand why it is so important to eat wholesome foods and how to personalize your nutrition according to your needs. This includes anti-aging, anti-cancer and healing foods and herbs for many diseases. IT IS possible to get rid of your medications with nutritious food, natural remedies and a healthy lifestyle!

The second book will also tell the story of Judith's path of healing from cancer without any conventional treatment. As well, stories about our **journeys and adventures** will be included, with the most amazing photos taken by Wes.

### Check out "Mountains Deserts Oceans Photography" at www.mdo.photography.

The second book will also consider our beloved dogs. Most store bought dog foods are highly processed and made from the garbage of meat factories. There are a few brands that are human food grade and acceptable.

But the **healthiest choice is homemade**. We cook the majority of our dogs' food; it is easy to do, highly nutritious and they love it! Our oldest dog Edward is 13; he looks and behaves like a young puppy even while living with lyme disease.

# We would like to thank ...

*... everyone who supported our idea, giving advice and trying our recipes.*

*A special thanks to Niklas Kuehnel, a former "challenged cook", who is now turning into a chef. He was our "guinea pig ... if Nik can cook it – everybody can."*

*A special thanks to Judith's sister Lioba Franke who supported us with great ideas and tips!*

*We are grateful for the work of our friend Lisa Towson who not only supported with editing this book but also offered huge encouragement for the endeavour!*

WE LIVE MOSTLY ON OUR SAILBOAT
AND ONCE IN A WHILE DO ROAD
TRIPS WITH OUR CAMPER.

READ ABOUT OUR JOURNEY
WWW.SVHAKLUYT.COM

# TABLE OF CONTENTS

Book design by Anna Kremer and Dennis Frey

Editing by Lisa Towson

**DISCLAIMER**

This book is not intended to give medical advice.
This publication contains the opinions and ideas of the author and the publisher and is intended for
educational purposes only and not intended to diagnose or prescribe for any medical condition nor to
prevent, treat, mitigate or cure such conditions. The ideas and suggestions presented in this book do
not substitute a consult with your physician but is intended to help the reader make informed decisions
about their health. The author and the publisher expressly disclaim
any responsibility for any liability, loss or risk.

9 781778 277009